Instant

Bible Lessons for

Preschoolers

God's Servants Teach Me

by Pamela J. Kuhn

For information regarding the CPSIA on this printed material call:
203-595-3636 and provide reference # LANC-651218

rainbowpublishers®

An imprint of Rose Publishing, Inc.
Torrance, CA
www.Rose-Publishing.com

To Andrew Cessna, who is learning to be a servant of God.

INSTANT BIBLE LESSONS® FOR PRESCHOOLERS: GOD'S SERVANTS TEACH ME
©2014 by by Pamela J. Kuhn, seventeenth printing
ISBN 10: 1-885358-56-3
ISBN 13: 978-1-885358-56-1
Rainbow reorder #RB36852
RELIGION/Christian Ministry/Children

Rainbow Publishers
An imprint of Rose Publishing, Inc.
4733 Torrance Blvd., #259
Torrance, CA 90503
www.Rose-Publishing.com

Cover Design: Stray Cat Studio, San Diego, CA
Interior Illustrator: Chuck Galey

Scriptures are from the *Holy Bible: New International Version* (North American Edition), copyright ©1973, 1978, 1984 by the International Bible Society. Used by permission of Zondervan Bible Publishers.

Printed in the United States of America

Contents

Introduction 5
How to Use This Book 5

Chapter 1: Joshua Teaches Me to Be Brave 7
Brave Soldiers Chain 8
Glitter Verse 9
10 Marching Soldiers 10
Soldier Rations 11
Soldier Tic-Tac-Toe 12
Echoes of Bravery 13
Night-Time Fright 14
Marching to Canaan 15

Chapter 2: Nehemiah Teaches Me to Be Fair . . 17
Sing the Verse 18
Song Plates 19
Lacing Bear 20
Marshmallow Bear 21
Sad Nehemiah/Happy Nehemiah 22
Unhappy Builders 23
Help the Builders 24
Fair Games 25

Chapter 3: Stephen Teaches Me to Forgive . . . 27
What Should I Do? 28
Stephen's Stones 29
Stones for Me 30
Story Stones 31
Peanut Butter Stones 32
Stephen Puppet 33
Stones of Forgiveness 34
Forgiving Hearts 35

Chapter 4: The Wise Men Teach Me to Give . . 37
Giving Gifts 38
A Gift for Jesus 39
What Is Inside? 40
Musical Gift 41
Happy Birthday to Jesus 42
Giving Myself 43
Cheerful Giver Hanger 44
God's Gift to Us 45

Chapter 5: Ruth Teaches Me to Be Thankful . . 47
I Thank God 48
Gathering Wheat Puzzle 49

Helping Ruth 50
Cups of Thanks 51
Pray Thankfully 52
Thankful Worksheet 53
Ruth's Centerpiece 54
I'm Thankful For... 55

Chapter 6: Aaron Teaches Me to Be Helpful . . 57
Can I Be Helpful? 58
"I'll Do It" Cards 59
Helpful Hands Snack Cups 60
Helping Moses 61
It's a Handful 62
Handy Mobile 63
Cleaning Up 64
Finger Play 65

Chapter 7: David Teaches Me to Be Caring . . . 67
Show Compassion 68
Fit for a King 69
King David's Table 70
Kingly Crown 71
I'll Be a King, Too! 72
Sitting Pretty 73
Our Caring Class Poster 74
Hand Me the Scepter 75

Chapter 8: Philip Teaches Me to Tell Others
About Jesus 77
Tell the Good News 78
Good News Tattoos 79
Salt Painted Chariot 80
Handing Out the Good News 81
Match the Chariots 82
Are You Telling the Good News? 83
Chariot Wheels 84
Chariot Race 85

Chapter 9: Miscellaneous Activities
Be Willing Servants 87
God's Servants 88
Wiggle Buster for God's Servants 92
God's Servant Certificate 93
Help! 95
Who Am I? Review 96

Introduction

Can your preschoolers serve God? The Bible is full of examples of those who were servants of God. In *God's Servants Teach Me*, your preschoolers will learn about eight of God's servants. They will learn how they, too, can become servants of God.

Each of the first eight chapters includes a Bible story, memory verse and numerous activities to help reinforce the truth in the lesson. An additional chapter contains miscellaneous projects that can be used anytime throughout the study or at the end to "recap" the lesson. Teacher aids are also sprinkled throughout the book, including bulletin board ideas and discussion starters.

The most exciting aspect of *Instant Bible Lessons for Preschoolers*, which includes *I Belong to Jesus, God's Servants Teach Me, I Learn Respect* and *I Am God's Child,* is its flexibility. You can easily adapt these lessons to a Sunday school hour, a children's church service, a Wednesday night Bible study or family home use. And because there are a variety of reproducible ideas from which to choose, you will enjoy creating a class session that is best for your group of students, whether large or small, beginning or advanced, active or studious. Plus, the intriguing topics will keep your kids coming back for more, week after week.

This book is written to add fun and uniqueness to learning while reinforcing what it means to be a servant of God. Teaching children is exciting and rewarding, and in using *God's Servants Teach Me* you will find new joy in your heart as you realize you are a servant of God.

How to Use This Book

Each chapter begins with a Bible story which you may read to your class, followed by discussion questions. Then, use any or all of the activities in the chapter to help drive home the message of that lesson. All of the activities are tagged with one of the icons below, so you can quickly flip through the chapter and select the projects you need. Simply cut off the teacher instructions on the pages and duplicate as desired.

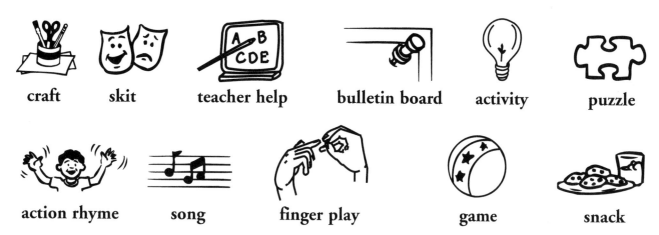

craft   skit   teacher help   bulletin board   activity   puzzle

action rhyme   song   finger play   game   snack

Chapter 1
Joshua Teaches Me to Be Brave

Memory Verse
Do not fear. Isaiah 35:4

Story to Share
Don't Be Afraid

The Israelites were wandering in the wilderness. God wanted His people to live in Canaan, but they would have to take the land from the Canannites.

"We're afraid. There are giants in that land," said one of the spies who had been sent to check out the land.

"That's right," said another spy. "We would be defeated."

Only two men, Joshua and Caleb, wanted to go fight the Canannites. They knew God would be with them. But the people of Israel were afraid so God punished them.

"You will wander in the wilderness for the rest of your lives. Only Joshua and Caleb, who believed I would be with them in war, will be brought into Canaan," said God.

When Moses, their leader, was dying, he called Joshua. "It is time for me to die. You will be the new leader. Take the people and go into Canaan. Don't be afraid. God will be with you."

When Moses died, God spoke to Joshua. "I want you to go and win the war against Canaan," He said. "Every place you walk I will give to My people."

Joshua knelt in the presence of God. "Yes, Lord."

Again God spoke. "I will be with you all the days of your life. I will never fail you, or leave you. Make sure you read the law I have written and obey it and I will be with you wherever you go."

Joshua went to his people and told them what God said. "God has given us a beautiful land to live in. It is Canaan—the land where wonderful crops will grow. The land has beautiful flowers blooming everywhere and strong, tall trees. We must go and possess the land. God wants us to be strong and not be afraid."

"Yes," agreed the people of Israel. "We will go. Whatever you say to us, we will do. We will not be afraid."

God gave Joshua and his people the land because they obeyed His voice and were not afraid.

— based on Joshua 1:1-18

Questions for Discussion
1. What are you afraid of?
2. Can God help you to be brave?

craft

· · · · · · · · · · ·

Materials

- soldier pattern
- safety scissors
- clear tape
- wiggle eyes
- red crayon

Directions

1. Fold 8 $\frac{1}{2}$" x 11" paper into fourths. Trace the soldier pattern on the top fourth, making sure the arms are touching the sides of the paper. Make one folded sheet for each student.
2. Assist the students in cutting on the lines, avoiding the folds.
3. Show the students where to glue the wiggle eyes and allow them to draw a smile.
4. Tape the children's soldiers together to form a long chain. Attach them to the wall for a classroom border.

Joshua Teaches Me to Be Brave

Brave Soldiers Chain

Glitter Verse

DO NOT FEAR

Isaiah 35:4

DO NOT FEAR

Isaiah 35:4

activity

- - - - - - - - - - -

Materials
- verse label
- glue in squeeze bottles
- glitter
- construction paper

Directions
1. Duplicate and cut out a verse label for each child. Cut a piece of construction paper 1" larger than the verse on all four sides.
2. Glue a verse to a construction paper rectangle for each child.
3. Show how to trace the verse with glue, one letter at a time, then sprinkle with glitter.

song

• • • • • • • • • •

Materials

- badges
- crayons
- spring-type clothespins
- glue

Directions

1. Before class, duplicate a badge for each child.
2. Allow the children to color the badges.
3. Assist in gluing a clothespin to the back of the badge. Clip the pin to the child's clothes.
4. Sing the song to the tune of "Ten Little Indians" while marching in place. If you have an open space, march in a circle.

10 Marching Soldiers

Song

1 marching, 2 marching, 3 marching soldiers.
4 marching, 5 marching, 6 marching soldiers.
7 marching, 8 marching, 9 marching soldiers.
10 brave soldiers march to war.

Soldier Rations

snack

· · · · · · · · · · ·

Materials

- cup wrap
- foam cups
- crayons
- glue
- grapes, bananas and apple slices

Directions

1. Before class, duplicate and cut out a cup wrap for each child.
2. Allow the children to color the cup wrap to look like camouflage material.
3. Demonstrate how to glue the wrap to the cup.
4. Fill the cups with fruit.
5. Say, **As you eat your snack, think about how brave the Israelites were to fight for their land. They were smart to do what God said. He helps us win battles if we ask Him.**

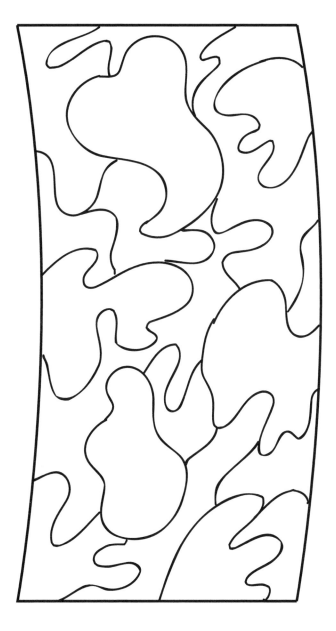

game

• • • • • • • • • • •

Materials

- Israelite and Canaanite figures
- light blue and yellow paper
- sticky tack

Directions

1. Before class, duplicate and cut out several Israelite figures from light blue paper and several Canaanites from yellow paper.
2. Draw a tic-tac-toe board on the blackboard or white board.
3. Place a small amount of sticky tack on the back of each soldier.
4. Divide the class into two teams. Ask the questions. For each correct answer one team member may put up a soldier. Three in a row wins!

Joshua Teaches Me to Be Brave

Soldier Tic-Tac-Toe

Questions

1. Where were the Israelites wandering?
2. Where did God want His people to live?
3. What did the spies say about the land after they had checked it out?
4. Who were the two men who wanted to go fight the Canaanites?
5. What was the punishment of the fearful men?
6. God told Joshua, "I will never _____ you."
7. Did the children of Israel listen to Joshua when he said, "We must go and fight?"
8. Were the children of Israel afraid?
9. Did God give Joshua and his people the land when they obeyed?

Answers

1. wilderness
2. Canaan
3. There were giants.
4. Joshua and Caleb
5. wander in the wilderness for the rest of life
6. leave
7. yes
8. no
9. yes

Echoes of Bravery

DO
NOT
FEAR

Isaiah 35:4

Materials
- verse helmet
- crayons
- glue
- paper plates
- dry beans
- craft sticks
- stapler
- clear tape

Directions
1. Before class, duplicate and cut out a helmet for each child.
2. Allow the children to color it.
3. Instruct the students to glue the helmet to the back of a paper plate.
4. Staple the plate together with a plain plate for each child. Insert a few beans inside and the craft stick at the bottom.
5. Cover the staples with clear tape to avoid injury.
6. March around the room, shaking the noisemaker and chanting, "Do not fear, Isaiah 35:4."

Usage
Allow the students to name fears they have. Add the fear to the chant: "Do not fear the dark," "Do not fear preschool" and so on.

Joshua Teaches Me to Be Brave

activity

Materials

- activity sheet
- black construction paper
- gold stars
- white crayons
- glue

Directions

1. Before class, duplicate the activity sheet for each child. Cut pieces of black construction paper to fit the activity sheet.
2. Show the children where to glue the construction paper to the worksheet.
3. Instruct them to use the white crayon to draw a picture of themselves in the dark.
4. Allow the children to stick stars in the darkness.
5. Say, **You may find the dark scary, but who is with you even in the dark?** (Jesus) **What does He say to us?** (Do not fear).

Joshua Teaches Me to Be Brave

Night-Time Fright

GLUE BLACK HERE

DO NOT FEAR
Isaiah 35:4

Marching to Canaan

puzzle

. . . .

Materials
- activity sheet
- crayons

Directions
1. Duplicate the activity sheet for each child.
2. Instruct the children to follow the marching footsteps from the wilderness to Canaan. Say, **Watch that you don't run into a scared soldier!**

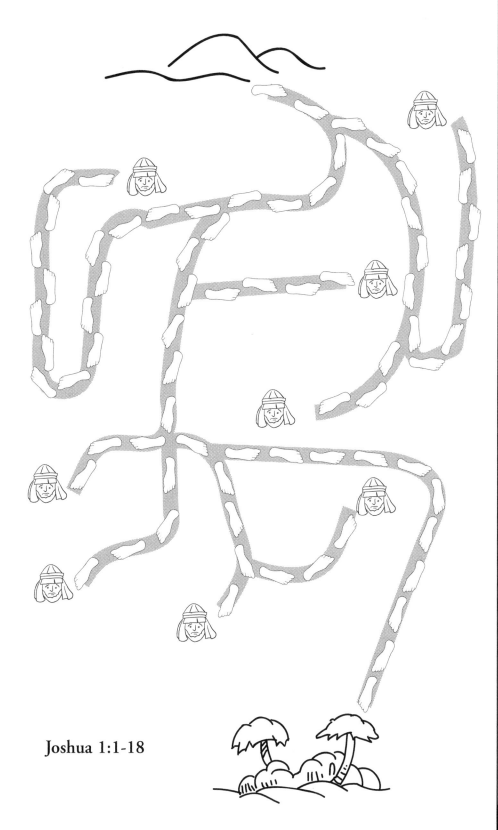

Joshua 1:1-18

Joshua Teaches Me to Be Brave

Chapter 2
Nehemiah Teaches Me to Be Fair

Memory Verse
Bear with each other. Colossians 3:13

Story to Share
Give It Back!

There was trouble in Jerusalem! The people were busy rebuilding the walls of Jerusalem under the leadership of Nehemiah. This was good, but the people were treating each other badly.

The rich men were being mean to the poor. There was no food in Jerusalem because their enemies were able to get through the broken walls and steal all their crops. The poor were desperate for food.

"I'll give you food," said one rich man. "But you must give me your land if you can't pay."

When the poor couldn't pay the rich what they owed them, they forced the poor man's sons and daughters to become their slaves. The rich took their vineyards and lands so the poor couldn't work to get their families back.

"Help, us, Nehemiah," they cried.

Nehemiah was angry. "What you are doing is not good," he told the rich men. "It is not fair for you to take the land and vineyards that belong to others. You should give back the houses, land and money."

The rich hung their heads. "Yes, Nehemiah, we will obey. We will give back what belongs to them."

Nehemiah called the priest. "Give the priest a promise that you will do what you have said."

Then Nehemiah shook his robe. "May God shake each of you out of your homes and lands who doesn't keep his promise, just as I shook out my robe."

"Amen!" God's people said. "We have learned to be fair. Praise the Lord."

— based on Nehemiah 5:1-19

Questions for Discussion
1. Who was unfair in our story?
2. Who told them what they were doing was wrong?
3. Who is our leader who tells us when we are wrong?

Materials
- bear
- brown construction paper
- hole punch
- glue
- cotton swabs

Directions
1. Duplicate a bear for each child.
2. Allow the students to punch holes in brown construction paper, creating confetti circles.
3. Show how to use cotton swabs to spread glue on the bear and drop the brown circles into the glue, being careful not to glue on the verse.
4. Say, **You made a bear to remind you to "Bear with each other."**

Sing the Verse

Bear with each other

Colossians 3:13

Song Plates

activity/ song

. . . .

Materials
- bear and friend patterns
- crayons
- glue
- 6" paper plates
- craft sticks
- stapler
- clear tape

Directions
1. Before class, duplicate and cut out a bear and friend for each child.
2. Allow the children to color the bear and friend.
3. Instruct the children to glue the bear to the back of one paper plate and the friend to the back of the other.
4. Sandwich the craft stick between the paper plates and staple them together for the children. Cover the staples with clear tape to avoid injury.
5. Sing the song to the tune of "Stop and Let Me Tell You." Show the children how to hold up the bear and then to turn the plates for "with all your friends."

Song

Bear with one another and with all your friends be fair.
Bear with one another and with all your friends be fair.
Don't grrrrowl, grrrrowl, grrrrowl, like a big, big bear.
Wear a smiley face and always share.
Bear with each other and with all your friends be fair.

Nehemiah Teaches Me to Be Fair

Lacing Bear

activity

. . . .

Materials
- bear
- poster board
- shoestrings
- hole punch

Directions

1. Before class, duplicate the bear pattern and trace it onto poster board. Cut out one per student. Punch holes around the perimeter of the bear as indicated.
2. Instruct the children to lace the bear.

Discuss

Say, **Nehemiah wanted the rich men to be fair with those who needed their land back. What if the rich men would need help with a chore? Do you think it would be fair of those who had been given back their land to help? Being fair goes both ways. We should bear with each other.**

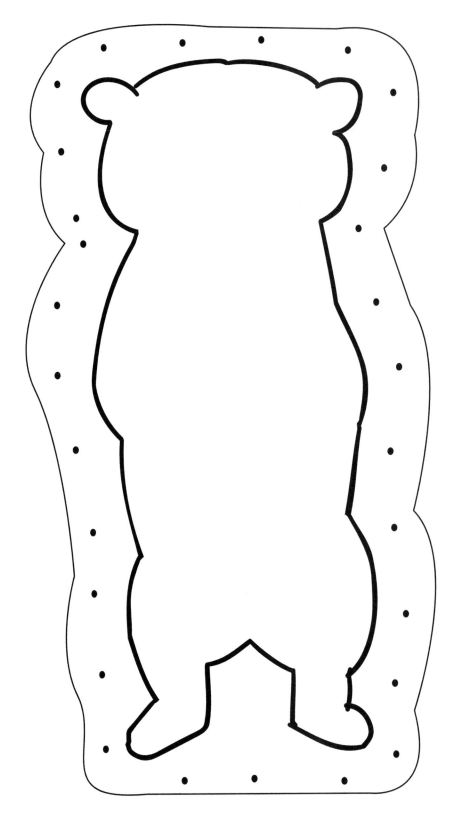

Marshmallow Bear

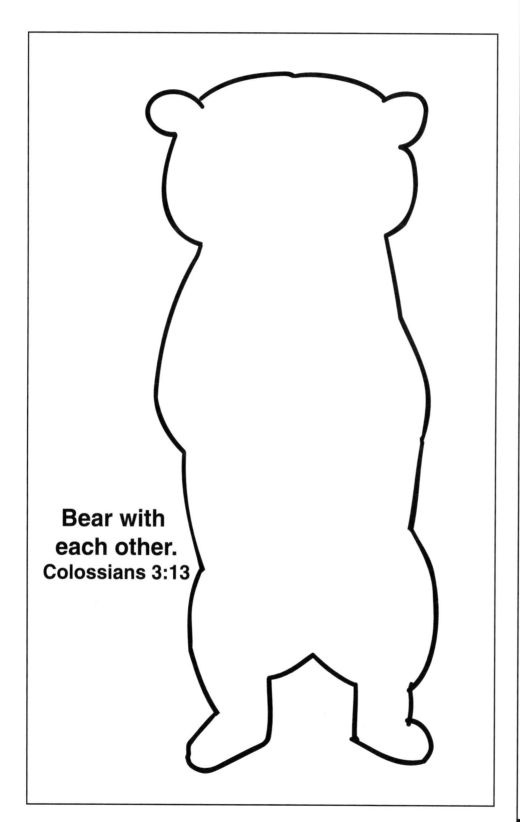

Bear with each other.
Colossians 3:13

Materials
- bear mat
- clear, self-stick paper
- large marshmallows
- miniature marshmallows
- chocolate chips
- mini candy-coated chocolate candies

Directions
1. Before class, duplicate and cut out a placemat for each child. Cover with clear, self-stick plastic.
2. Give each child two large marshmallows, two small marshmallows, two chocolate chips and two chocolate candies.
3. Instruct the children to flatten the large marshmallows, flattening one more than the other.
4. Show how to follow the placemat guide, using the larger marshmallow for the body of the bear and the flattened one for the head. Use the two small marshmallows for ears, chips for eyes and candies for buttons.

Nehemiah Teaches Me to Be Fair

Sad Nehemiah/Happy Nehemiah

Materials
- face and features
- crayons
- glue

Directions
1. Before class, duplicate and cut out the nose, eyes and mouths for each child.
2. Allow the children to color the eyes and mouths.
3. Instruct the children to glue the eyes and nose where indicated on the face.
4. Show how to insert the mouth strip into the slit.
5. Say the poem at right, instructing the children to change Nehemiah from sad to happy.

Nehemiah Teaches Me to Be Fair

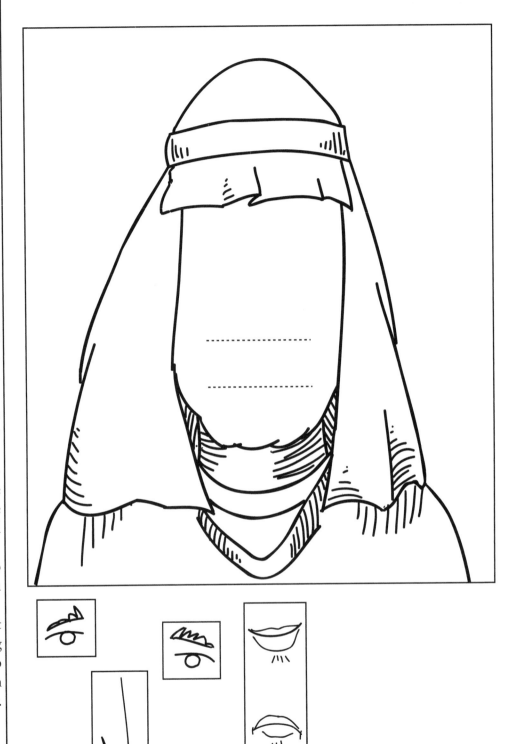

Poem

In Jerusalem, Nehemiah was very sad.
The rich weren't being fair—not a tad!
They said, "We are sorry we were bad,"
Which made Nehemiah very, very glad.

Unhappy Builders

puzzle

• • • • • • • • • •

Materials
- activity sheet
- crayons
- smiley face stickers

Directions
1. Before class, duplicate an activity sheet for each child.
2. Say, **The people who were rebuilding the walls of Jerusalem were not happy because of the way the rich were treating them. When Nehemiah encouraged the rich men to be fair, the poor people's frowns turned upside-down.**
3. Instruct the children to find ten frowning faces and stick a smiley face sticker on each one.
4. Allow the children to color the rest of the picture.

Nehemiah Teaches Me to Be Fair

activity

Materials

- activity sheet
- crayons

Directions

1. Before class, duplicate the activity sheet for each child.
2. Instruct the children to help the builders finish the wall by drawing it.
3. Allow the children to color the picture.

Help the Builders

Fair Games

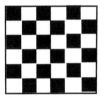

Materials

- activity sheet
- crayons

Directions

1. Before class, duplicate the activity sheet for each child.
2. Say, **When you play games you need to play fair. Cheating does not make Jesus happy. Many times others may not play as well as you. Remember, "Bear with each other!"**
3. Instruct the children to match the games by drawing lines between them.

Nehemiah Teaches Me to Be Fair

25

Chapter 3
Stephen Teaches Me to Forgive

Memory Verse
Forgive as the Lord forgave you. Colossians 3:13

Story to Share
It's Okay

After Jesus went away to heaven, the disciples were faithful to tell others that Jesus could save them from their sins. The number of Christians was growing every day. The disciples couldn't take care of everyone, so they appointed seven men to help. One of the men was Stephen.

Stephen was a wise man. He was close to God and God was able to work many miracles through him. Stephen was a great preacher, too. Some of the Jewish leaders didn't like Stephen because of the many people who followed him. They arrested him and brought him before the council.

"This man has spoken against God and Moses," they said. "He deserves to be punished."

The council questioned Stephen. "Did you say Jesus would destroy the temple? Did you say you wanted to change the laws of Moses?"

As the high priest waited for Stephen to answer, he looked at his face. His eyes opened wide in surprise. Stephen's face looked shiny and calm—just like an angel's face.

"You will not listen to what God wants. Jesus came to save you and you killed Him," Stephen told the council.

This made the people even angrier. They covered their ears so they wouldn't have to hear what he was preaching. The men grabbed Stephen, dragging him out of the city walls, and then began throwing stones at him.

As the stones pounded against his body, Stephen prayed, "It's okay, God. Don't hold this against these people. I forgive them." And then Stephen died.

— based on Acts 6:8-15; 7:54-60

Questions for Discussion
1. Why did the men hate Stephen?
2. Should you forgive your friends when they are mean to you?

What Should I Do?

activity/ song

. . . .

Materials
- cross
- wood shavings
- glue

Directions
1. Duplicate the cross picture for each child.
2. Instruct the students to glue wood shavings to the cross.
3. Sing the song to the tune of "If You're Happy and You Know It."

Stephen Teaches Me to Forgive

Song

If someone punches your nose then forgive. FORGIVE!!   *hold nose*

If someone steps on your toes then forgive. FORGIVE!   *point to toes*

God forgave you, in return you forgive.   *hold up cross*

Be like Stephen and don't get mad, just forgive. FORGIVE!   *shake head*

28

Stephen's Stones

Materials
- activity sheet
- small pieces of gravel
- glue
- crayons

Directions
1. Before class, duplicate the activity sheet for each child.
2. Allow the children to color the picture.
3. Count out pieces of gravel to match the number and glue to each spot.
4. Ask, **What did Stephen do even though the men threw stones at him?**

Stephen Teaches Me to Forgive

29

Stones for Me

activity

. . . .

Materials
- activity sheet
- cotton balls
- crayons
- glue

Directions

1. Before class, duplicate the activity sheet for each child. Cut out the stones.

2. Instruct the children to color the stones and draw their faces on the child on the worksheet.

3. Show the children how to glue cotton balls to the Xs then glue the stones on top of them.

4. Ask, **What should you do if someone hits you? What should you do if someone makes fun of you? What should you do if someone won't let you play with his toy? The cotton reminds us that we should be nice, not throw stones.**

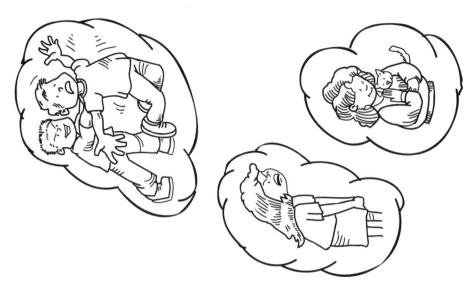

Forgive as the Lord forgave you. Colossians 3:13

Story Stones

craft

• • • • • • • • • • •

Materials
- story pictures and plain stones
- gray paper
- crayons
- hole punch
- yarn
- craft sticks

Directions
1. Before class, duplicate and cut out the story pictures from white paper. Duplicate and cut out the stones from gray paper. Punch holes at the tops of the gray stones. Make one set of each for every student.
2. Allow the children to color the story pictures.
3. Have the students glue the story pictures on the gray stones.
4. Help the children put the story in order and tie yarn through the holes.
5. Show how to glue a craft stick to the back of the story stones as a holder.
6. Say, **When someone hurts you, tell the story of Stephen and remember, FORGIVE!**

Stephen Teaches Me to Forgive

Peanut Butter Stones

. . . .
Materials

- victory flag
- crayons
- blunt-end toothpicks
- 1/2 cup peanut butter
- 3/4 cup powdered sugar
- 3/4 cup dry milk
- 1/2 cup corn syrup
- mini chocolate chips

Directions

1. Before class, duplicate and cut several flags for each child.
2. Allow the students to color the flags. Show how to fold and glue them around the toothpicks.
3. Mix the peanut butter, sugar, milk and syrup together. Knead in the chips.
4. Give some to the children and instruct them to roll it into round stones.
5. Allow the children to stick the flags in the stones until they are ready to eat them.
6. Ask, **Do you remember what Stephen did when the stones hit him? He prayed: "Forgive them." He pleased Jesus by telling others about Him.**

Stephen Teaches Me to Forgive

Stephen Puppet

craft/activity

• • • • • • • • • • •

Materials
• Stephen face
• crayons
• glue
• paper lunch sack

Directions
1. Before class, duplicate and cut out a Stephen face for each child.
2. Allow the children to color their Stephen.
3. Show the students where to glue Stephen to the paper sack.
4. Read the script at left, allowing the children to use their puppets to say the part of Stephen. You may wish to point to the children so they will know it is their turn. You may also point to one child indicating that he or she is the one to say, "Forgive these men."

finished craft

Teacher:	The religious officials were angry. Stephen was preaching about Jesus.
Students:	Forgive these men.
Teacher:	Stephen was arrested and brought before the council.
Students:	Forgive these men.
Teacher:	Stephen preached to the council. The men became even angrier.
Students:	Forgive these men.
Teacher:	They grabbed Stephen, dragged him out of the city walls and began throwing stones at him.
Students:	Forgive these men.
Teacher:	As Stephen was dying, his last words were…
Students:	Forgive these men.

game

• • • • • • • • • •

Materials

- stones, front and back
- glue
- cotton balls
- two empty milk cartons

Directions

1. Cut the tops off of two empty paper milk cartons.
2. Duplicate and cut out two fronts and backs of stones.
3. Place a cotton ball in the middle of each stone back. Place the stone front on top, glue them together along the edges and press front to back. Allow to dry.
4. Divide the children into two teams. The teams should stand in line, single file.
5. Place the cartons one foot in front of the first child. At the go signal the first two should try to throw the stone into the carton, then run to the back of the line. Continue until one team is finished. The team with the most stones in the carton wins.

Stones of Forgiveness

FORGIVE
Colossians 3:13

FORGIVE
Colossians 3:13

Forgiving Hearts

Forgive as the Lord forgave you.
Colossians 3:13

Materials
- activity sheet
- crayons

Directions
1. Before class, duplicate an activity sheet for each child.
2. Say, **Even while the stones were hitting Stephen, he was sending forgiveness back to the sinful men.**
3. Instruct the students to circle ten forgiving hearts, then color the picture.

Memory Verse
God loves a cheerful giver. 2 Corinthians 9:7

Story to Share
Gifts for Jesus

"Laben," said one of the wise men, looking up at the stars. "Laben, come quickly. There's a new star in the sky."

Laben hurried over to where his friends Simon and David were looking toward heaven. "Where, what kind of star?"

David pointed. "There, it's the brightest star I've ever seen," he said quietly.

The wise men stared at the star. It WAS the brightest star they had ever seen. It was telling them that a king had been born. Without delay, the wise men prepared for the journey. They would take gifts to this new king, and worship Him.

For long days the men traveled. They grew tired and eager to reach their destination. Over and over they talked about the king of the Jews—the tiny baby whose star they had seen.

One day, Mary heard loud noises. Rushing to the window she gasped in surprise. Camels? And who were these men riding them? They looked like important men, at least rich men. Their robes were colorful and made of the finest fabrics.

Mary watched in amazement as the men asked permission to see the baby, the king of the Jews. Tears filled her eyes as each of these important guests bowed on their knees and worshipped her son.

Simon handed Joseph a gift. "This is my gift to the baby Jesus. It is gold to show He is King."

Laben handed Joseph his gift. "My gift to your son is frankincense. This incense is burned to make the air sweet in honor to God. Somehow this baby is both man and God."

Bowing his head, David offered his gift. "My gift is myrrh, a special perfume worn only by important men. It is also used to prepare men for burial." Somehow David knew this God who had become man would die.

Mary and Joseph tried to thank the wise men for their gifts. "You have given your gifts so willingly. May you be blessed."

Bowing low, the wise men once again worshipped Jesus.

— based on Matthew 2:1-14

Questions for Discussion
1. What would you give as a gift to baby Jesus?
2. What should your face look like when you give?

Giving Gifts

activity/song

• • • • • • • • • • •

Materials

• gift wrap pattern
• crayons
• clear tape
• ribbon
• wood blocks or small boxes

Directions

1. Duplicate the gift wrap for each student.
2. Allow the children to color the wrapping paper.
3. Assist the students as they wrap a block of wood or box and tie it with a ribbon.
4. Instruct the children to sit in a circle. Sing the song to tune of "Frère Jacques." At each verse the children should take turns putting their gifts in the center of the circle.

The Wise Men Teach Me to Give

Song

Giving gifts, giving gifts, to my friends, to my friends.
I will share my toys,
With the girls and boys,
Giving gifts, giving gifts.

Giving gifts, giving gifts, to my friends, to my friends.
Putting books upon the shelf,
Giving of myself,
Giving gifts, giving gifts.

Giving gifts, giving gifts, to my friends, to my friends.
Taking pretty flowers,
To my lonely neighbor,
Giving gifts, giving gifts.

A Gift for Jesus

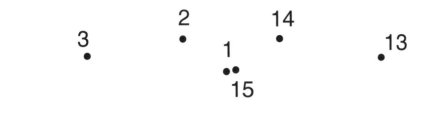

3   2   14   13
   1
15

4

5

6   12

     11

   10

7   9

8

God loves a cheerful giver.
2 Corinthians 9:7

Materials
- activity sheet
- crayons

Directions
1. Before class, duplicate an activity sheet for each child.
2. Say, **Follow the dots to see what gift you can give to Jesus.**
3. Allow the children to color the heart.

What Is Inside?

. . . .

Materials
- activity sheet
- crayons

Directions

1. Before class, duplicate the activity sheet for each child.
2. Say, **The wise men gave gifts to Jesus. You can give Jesus your heart.**
3. Show children how to match the gifts on the left with the outlines of them around the wise men's gifts on the right by drawing lines.
4. The students may color the picture.

The Wise Men Teach Me to Give

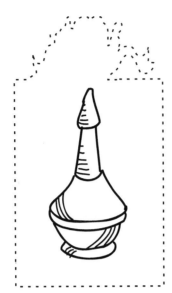
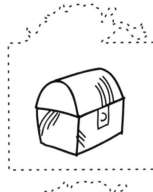

Musical Gift

game

. . . .

Materials

- package top and tag
- markers
- gift bow
- glue
- small box
- music tape
- tape player

Directions

1. Cut out the package top and tag.
2. Color the holly and berries on the package top. Glue it to the top of the box.
3. Put a bow on top. Glue the tag to the box.
4. Make a circle with chairs. The students should pass the box around while the music plays. The one who has the gift when the music stops should stand and say the memory verse with the teacher. Continue until the verse has been learned by all.

GOD LOVES A
CHEERFUL GIVER.

2 Corinthians 9:7

**The Wise Men
Teach Me to Give**

41

Happy Birthday to Jesus

snack

• • • • • • • • • • •

Materials
- birthday candle pattern
- poster board
- crayons
- paper muffin cups
- popcorn

Directions
1. Before class, cut a birthday candle from poster board for each child.
2. Allow the children to color both sides of the candle and flame.
3. Fill the muffin cups with popcorn.
4. Have everyone slide their candles in their popcorn cups and sing "Happy Birthday to Jesus" before enjoying the snack.

Usage
Children love to watch popcorn pop. But be careful—it can be very hot. Allow them to watch at a safe distance.

The Wise Men Teach Me to Give

Giving Myself

God loves a
cheerful giver.
2 Corinthians 9:7

I'd like to give
you a gift

You are
so special

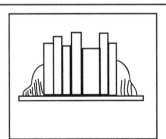

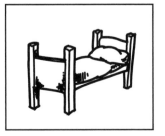

Materials
- card and gift pic-
  tures
- glue
- crayons

Directions
1. Before class, dupli-
   cate, cut out and
   pre-fold a card
   for each student.
   Duplicate and cut
   out several gifts so
   the students may
   select one.
2. Say, **You can give
   a gift of yourself
   to your parents
   this week. Look
   at the gifts and
   choose the one
   you want to give
   to your parents.**
3. Instruct the chil-
   dren to choose the
   gift they want to
   give.
4. Allow the children
   to glue the gift to
   the card, then
   color it.

**The Wise Men
Teach Me to Give**

craft

· · · · · · · · · · ·

Materials

- gift patterns
- crayons
- yarn
- glue

Directions

1. Before class, duplicate and cut out a set of gift patterns for each child.
2. Allow the children to color the gift patterns.
3. Show how to glue the front and back of the gift together with a loop of yarn between them for a hanger.

Cheerful Giver Hanger

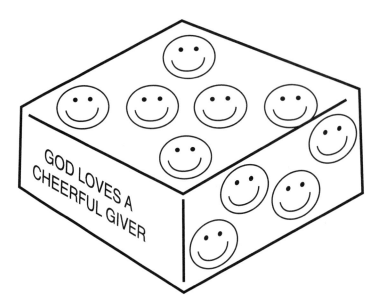

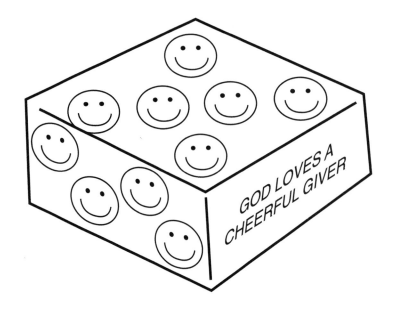

God's Gift to Us

. . . .
Materials
- activity sheet
- crayons

Directions
1. Before class, duplicate an activity sheet for each child.
2. Ask, **What do you think is God's gift to us? Color the picture to find out.**
3. Instruct the students to color all of the spaces with one dot brown; spaces with two dots yellow and spaces with three dots blue.

Matthew 2:1-14

The Wise Men Teach Me to Give

45

Chapter 5
Ruth Teaches Me to Be Thankful

Memory Verse
Give thanks to him. Psalm 100:4

Story to Share
Thank You, Thank You!

Ruth and Naomi were moving. They were moving from Moab to Bethlehem. "Ruth, my dear daughter-in-law, you do not need to move with me," said Naomi. "You have lived in Moab all your life."

"Naomi," said Ruth, "I am moving with you. When I married your son I learned to love the same God you serve. Now my husband is dead, but I love you and I want to move with you back to Bethlehem."

The two women traveled on, finally reaching the town that sat up on a hill. What excitement there was in the little town when the people saw Naomi.

"Naomi! We're so glad to see you," said one.

"Naomi, it's good to see you back home where you belong," another told her.

Naomi was so glad to be back in Bethlehem. But there was the responsibility of finding food for the two of them. "Naomi, don't you worry about our food," Ruth told her. "It's the time of barley harvest. You have told me the Israelites always leave some grain standing for the poor. I'll go to the fields tomorrow and gather the barley that is left."

Boaz owned the fields where Ruth went to pick the barley. He had heard how kind she had been to travel all the distance with Naomi and take care of her.

"Come and eat our food for lunch," said Boaz. "You will be safe here and you may gather all the barley you need."

Ruth's heart was happy because of Boaz's kindness. "Thank you, thank you," she told him.

That night, when Ruth told Naomi what Boaz had said, Naomi said, "Ruth, let us thank God for taking care of us."

Together the two women thanked God for being so good to them. "Thank you, God, thank you," Ruth said again.

— based on Ruth 2:8-17

Questions for Discussion
1. What has God done for you that you are thankful for?
2. How can we show our thanks?

I Thank God

activity/song

• • • • • • • • • • •

Materials
• thankful circle
• 9" paper plates
• crayons
• glue
• magnets

Directions
1. Before class, duplicate and cut out a thankful circle for each child.
2. Ask, **What is your favorite food to eat? Draw a picture of it in the middle of the thankful circle.**
3. Instruct the children to glue the circle to the middle of a paper plate.
4. Show how to make stripes with crayons around the frame of the plate.
5. Give each child a magnet to glue on the back of the plate.
6. Sing the song to the tune of "Sing a Song of Sixpence."
7. Instruct the children to stand up on "standing on my feet," holding their plates as high as possible.

Ruth Teaches Me to Be Thankful

GIVE THANKS TO HIM

Psalm 100:4

Song

Ruth was very thankful for her grains of wheat.

I think her example could not be beat.

So I will thank my God, while standing on my feet,

I love all the food He gives…from potatoes to the meat!

Gathering Wheat Puzzle

puzzle

. . . .

Materials
- puzzle pieces and board
- poster board
- meat trays
- crayons
- safety scissors
- foam meat trays

Directions
1. Before class, duplicate and cut out two puzzles for each child.
2. Allow the children to color one.
3. Show how to cut the colored one apart on the lines.
4. Instruct the students to glue the plain one on the meat tray.
5. Show how to put the puzzle together on the puzzle board.

**Give thanks to him.
Psalm 100:4**

Helping Ruth

game

• • • • • • • • • • •

Materials
• food cards
• two baskets

Directions
1. Before class, duplicate and cut out the food cards. You may need two sets of cards.
2. Divide the children into two teams, lining the teams in single file position.
3. Choose one child from each team to be Ruth. Ruth should sit on the ground ten feet away from the line with a basket in her lap.
4. Place the food cards in a box between the two teams.
5. At the go signal, the first in line should grab a food card, run to Ruth and say, "I am thankful for [name of food on card]," drop the card in the basket and run back to tag the hand of the next person in line. Continue until one team finishes.
6. The first team to finish gets 5 bonus points. Add up the points to see which team wins.

Ruth Teaches Me to Be Thankful

Cups of Thanks

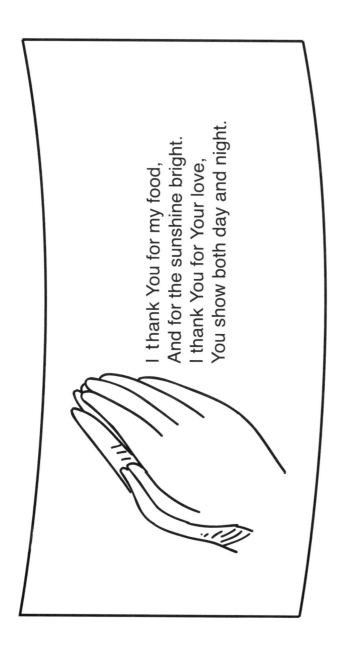

I thank You for my food,
And for the sunshine bright.
I thank You for Your love,
You show both day and night.

snack

. . . .

Materials
- prayer label
- glue
- paper cups
- crayons
- pudding
- cookie crumbles
- spoons

Directions
1. Before class, duplicate and cut out a prayer label for each child.
2. Instruct the children to glue the prayer to the front of the cup.
3. Fill the cups with pudding and allow the children to sprinkle cookie crumbs on top.
4. Read the prayer twice, then ask the children to pray the prayer with you before they eat their snack.

Ruth Teaches Me to Be Thankful

Pray Thankfully

activity

. . . .

Materials

- activity sheet
- poster board
- glue
- heavy-duty aluminum foil
- yarn

Directions

1. Before class, duplicate the activity sheet on poster board for each child.
2. Say, **When you pray, do not only ask God for what you want or need. Be sure to thank God for all He has given you.**
3. Show how to trace around the praying hands with glue. Allow to dry.
4. While the hands dry, allow the children to name blessings from God.
5. Give each child a piece of foil, slightly larger than the worksheet. Show how to cover the sheet with foil, smoothing it down around the edges and over the glue ridges.
6. Tape a yarn loop to the back of each child's sheet for hanging.

Ruth Teaches Me to Be Thankful

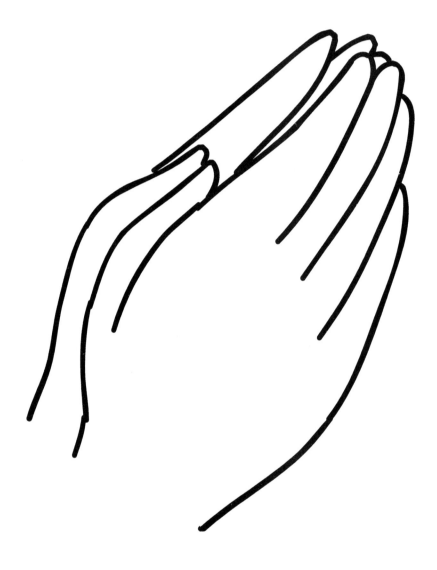

52

Thankful Worksheet

Give thanks to him.
Psalm 100:4

puzzle

. . . .

Materials
• activity sheet
• crayons

Directions
1. Before class, duplicate the activity sheet for each child.
2. Instruct the children to circle the picture that is different.
3. Allow the children to color the picture.

Usage
Say, **It looks like Ruth, Naomi and Boaz all knew the memory verse, "Give thanks to him."**

Ruth Teaches Me to Be Thankful

53

craft

• • • • • • • • • •

Materials

- vase wrap
- plastic soda bottles
- ribbon
- glue
- crayons
- wheat or other long plant

Directions

1. Before class, duplicate and cut out a vase wrap for each child. If wheat is not available in your area, use pretend "wheat," such as long grass or weeds.
2. Allow the children to color the vase wrap.
3. Instruct them to glue the wrap around the bottle.
4. Assist the students in tying a ribbon around the top of the bottle.
5. Allow the children to insert "wheat" into vase.

Ruth Teaches Me to Be Thankful

Ruth's Centerpiece

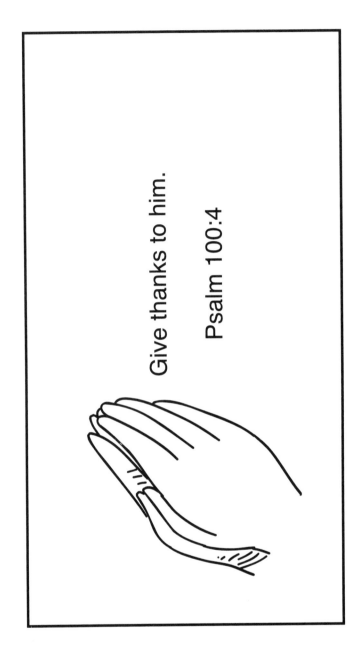

Give thanks to him.

Psalm 100:4

I'm Thankful For...

. . . .

Materials
• activity sheet
• crayons

Directions
1. Before class, duplicate an activity sheet for each child.
2. Instruct the children to draw what they are thankful for in the prayer cloud.
3. Allow the students to color the picture.

Usage
Discuss with the children the things they are thankful for. Ask, **Do you have a pet you are thankful for? A bed you slept in last night? Do you like the warm sunshine or the twinkling stars?**

Give thanks to him.
Psalm 100:4

Ruth Teaches Me to Be Thankful

Chapter 6
Aaron Teaches Me to Be Helpful

Memory Verse

Be devoted to one another. Romans 12:10

Story to Share
We'll Help You, Moses

Moses called Joshua to his tent. "Joshua," he said, "the Amalekites are causing problems for us. We need to fight them. God has shown me that you are to choose some men for us who are good soldiers. Take the men and go out against Amalek and his army."

"I will, Moses," said Joshua. "Is that all God said?"

"No. God told me to stand at the top of the hill while you are fighting. I will hold the rod of God in my hands, lifting it toward heaven."

Early the next morning, Joshua obediently gathered his men together and went to fight. Moses went to the top of the hill with Aaron and Hur. Moses lifted the rod toward God and the fighting began.

The Amalekites were good warriors. But they were no match for God. The Israelites were winning the war. As they fought, Moses' hands began to get tired. "I think I will rest my hands for a moment, Aaron," he said. Resting the rod on the ground, Moses shook his arms, but noticed with dismay that the Amalekites were beginning to gain ground.

Quickly, Moses raised his arms again and the Israelites pushed the Amalekites back. "Aaron, did you see that?" asked Moses.

"Yes, Moses," he said, "you need to keep the rod raised."

"I will try," Moses answered, "but my arms are so heavy and tired."

Aaron rolled a large stone over to where Moses was standing. "Sit down, Moses, and rest. Hur and I will support your arms."

All day Aaron and Hur helped Moses. His hands held high the rod of the Lord toward heaven. When the sun went down that night, Amalek was defeated.

"Thank you, Aaron and Hur," said Moses. "Thank you for helping me hold my hands up to God. Because of you, Joshua defeated Amalek and his people with the edge of his sword."

— based on Exodus 17:8-16

Questions for Discussion

1. Do you think Aaron and Hur helped Moses cheerfully?
2. What can you do to be helpful today?

Can I Be Helpful?

song

• • • • • • • • • • •

Materials
• activity sheet

Directions
1. Before class, duplicate the activity sheet for each child.
2. Sing the song to the tune of "The Bear Went Over the Mountain."
3. The boys should stand and sing the first verse, the girls the second.
4. Take time at the end of the song to listen to what the children can do to be helpful, then say, **Those are good ideas, why don't you draw what you can do to be helpful on your worksheet?**

<u>Song</u>

Do you think I can be helpful?
Do you think I can be helpful?
Do you think I can be helpful,
If I'm just a little boy?   *bow*

Do you think I can be helpful?
Do you think I can be helpful?
Do you think I can be helpful,
If I'm just a little girl?   *curtsy*

Can I empty the stinky trash?
Can I empty the stinky trash?
Can I empty the stinky trash,
Although I'm very small?   *hold nose*

Can I clean my messy room?
Can I clean my messy room?
Can I clean my messy room,
Although I'm very small?   *sweeping motions*

What can I do to be helpful?
What can I do to be helpful?
What can I do to be helpful,
Although I'm very small?   *hands out, palms up*

"I'll Do It" Cards

craft

DEVOTED TO ONE ANOTHER
Romans 12:10

Materials

- helping cards and verse
- heavy paper
- crayons
- plastic drinking straws
- envelopes
- stapler
- clear tape

Directions

1. Before class, duplicate and cut out the helping cards and verse for each child. Copy the helping cards on heavy paper.
2. Allow the children to color the helping cards.
3. Staple the cards to the straws. Cover the staples with tape to avoid injury.
4. Instruct the children to seal the envelope. Slit one side of each envelope. show how to stick the straws, card side down, in the envelope.
5. Have the children glue the verse card to the front of the envelope.
6. Say, **Each day you may pull out one of your straws and be helpful by doing the chore on the card.**

Aaron Teaches Me to Be Helpful

Helpful Hands Snack Cups

snack

• • • • • • • • • • •

Materials

- hands and verse
- glue
- paper cups
- pink paint
- paint brushes
- paint smocks

Directions

1. Duplicate and cut out the hands and verse for each child. Mix the paint and glue together at a 1:1 ratio.
2. Help the children into paint smocks. Allow the children to paint the paper hands.
3. While the small hand is still wet, press the verse into the paint.
4. Instruct the children to glue the hands to the paper cup, small in front and large in back.
5. Choose some helpful hands to fill the cups with tiny cookies, raisins and pretzels.

Usage

This is a good craft to do at the beginning of your class. When it is time for snacks the hands will be dry and may be glued to the cup.

Aaron Teaches Me to Be Helpful

Be
devoted
to one
another

Helping Moses

Materials
• activity sheet
• crayons
• safety scissors

Directions
1. Before class, duplicate an activity sheet for each child.
2. Allow the children to color the circle puzzle.
3. Assist in cutting out the circle puzzles for the children.

Aaron Teaches Me to Be Helpful

61

It's a Handful

Materials
• story pictures
• craft sticks
• construction paper
• glue
• crayons
• safety scissors

Directions
1. Before class, duplicate and cut out the story pictures for each child.
2. Assist the children in tracing around their hands and cutting them out.
3. Show how to glue around the hands and press them together, leaving the wrist part open.
4. Allow the children to color the story pictures and glue them to the craft sticks.
5. Instruct the children to put the story pictures in the hand and use them to tell the story to others.

Aaron Teaches Me to Be Helpful

Handy Mobile

craft

. . . .

Materials
- mobile pieces
- crayons
- heavy thread
- tape

Directions
1. Before class, duplicate and cut out one set of mobile pieces for each student.
2. Allow the children to color the happy hands.
3. Assist the children in taping thread on the mobile top and on the hands.
4. Make a small hole at the top of the mobile for hanging.

BE DEVOTED TO ONE ANOTHER
Romans 12:10

Cleaning Up

Materials

- trash hands
- crayons
- glue
- paper trash bags

Directions

1. Before class, duplicate and cut out the trash hands for each child.
2. Allow the children to color the trash hands.
3. Instruct the children to glue the hands to the front of a trash bag.
4. Say, **Keeping God's world clean is a good way to have helping hands. Use your bag to pick up trash on the street on which you live.**

Keep
God's
World
Clean

Finger Play

finger play

• • • • • • • • • •

Directions

1. As you say each line, act out the words with your hands.
2. After you do the finger play once, have the children join you.

Usage

Allow the children to suggest ways to use their helping hands.

I use my helping hands,
To pick up all my toys.
One, two, three.
Can you see?

I use my helping hands,
To pick the pretty flowers.
One, two, three.
Can you see?

I use my helping hands,
To sweep up the leaves.
One, two, three.
Can you see?

Chapter 7
David Teaches Me to Be Caring

Memory Verse

Show...compassion to one another. Zechariah 7:9

Story to Share
David Cares for a Friend

Jonathan, King Saul's son, was David's best friend. They loved each other as much as they loved themselves.

"David," promised Jonathan, "I will be your friend for life."

"Thank you, Jonathan," said David. "You will always be my friend, too. I will always be kind to you and your family."

Many years passed and King Saul and his son died. David was crowned king over Israel. One day King David was remembering the friendship of Jonathan. He called one of his servants to him.

"Is there anyone left from Jonathan's family?" he asked.

"There is one, Mephibosheth, a son of Jonathan. He is crippled in both feet from a fall when he was young."

"Bring Mephibosheth to me," commanded King David.

Mephibosheth came before David. "Mephibosheth, I loved your father as my own self. I want to care for you to honor that love. I am going to give you all the land that belonged to your grandfather, King Saul. You will be like my son and eat all your meals with me at my table."

Because of the king's kindness, Mephibosheth became a wealthy man with much land. King David cared for Mephibosheth for the rest of his life.

— based on 2 Samuel 9:1-13

Questions for Discussion
1. Do you think Mephibosheth was happy that King David was caring for him?
2. Who can you make happy today?

Show Compassion

song

• • • • • • • • • • • •

Directions

1. Sing the song to the tune of "The Wheels on the Bus."
2. Instruct the children to pick a partner, face each other and hold hands. Pull back and forth to the rhythm of the music.

Song

Oh, show compassion to everyone, everyone, everyone.
Oh, show compassion to everyone,
That you see.

David cared for his friend's son, his friend's son, his friend's son.
David cared for his friend's son,
Compassion.

God wants us to show compassion, compassion, compassion,
God wants us to show compassion,
To everyone.

God shows compassion to you and me, you and me, you and me.
God shows compassion to you and me,
Yes, He cares!

Fit for a King

snack

• • • • • • • • • • •

Materials

- coaster square and crown
- poster board
- gold foil
- clear tape
- glue
- 1/2 cup orange-flavored fruit juice concentrate, thawed
- 4 cups of milk
- 2 cups of vanilla ice cream
- blender
- cups

Directions

1. Before class, duplicate and cut out the coaster square and crown for each student from poster board.
2. Instruct the children to glue the crown to the middle of the coaster square.
3. Show how to cover the front of the coaster with the foil, folding the excess foil around the edges. Tape in place.
4. Allow the children to press on the coaster front to make the outline of the crown.
5. Put the ingredients in the blender and mix on medium.
6. Pour into cups.

David Teaches Me to Be Caring

King David's Table

Materials

- activity sheet
- glue
- crayons

Directions

1. Before class, duplicate and cut out the scene, the food pictures and Mephibosheth.
2. Instruct the children to glue the food on the table.
3. Show the children where to glue Mephibosheth.
4. Allow the children to color the picture.

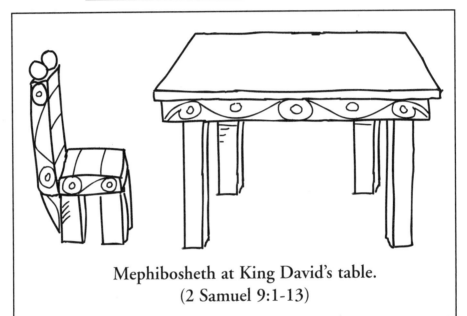

Mephibosheth at King David's table.
(2 Samuel 9:1-13)

Kingly Crown

Show...compassion to one another.
Zechariah 7:9

Materials
• crown and jewels
• colored foil
• crayons
• hole punch
• string
• glue

Directions
1. Before class, dupli-cate and cut out the crown from white paper. Duplicate the jewel patterns and use them to cut jewels from colored foil. Punch holes at both sides of the crown for the string.
2. Allow the children to color the crown.
3. Show where to glue the jewels.
4. Tie a string though the holes in each crown. Tie the crown around the child's head.

David Teaches Me to Be Caring

activity

. . . .

Materials
- activity sheet
- crayons

Directions
1. Duplicate the activity sheet for each child.
2. Instruct the children to draw their faces on the sheet.
3. Allow the children to color the picture.
4. Say, **You can be like King David by caring for your friends.**

I'll Be a King, Too!

Show…compassion to one another.
Zechariah 7:9

Sitting Pretty

· · · · · · · · · · ·

Materials
- activity sheet
- glue
- crayons
- gold glitter
- cotton swabs

Directions
1. Before class, duplicate the activity sheet and cut out the chair scene and Mephibosheth.
2. Allow the children to color the chair and Mephibosheth.
3. Show where to glue Mephibosheth to the chair.
4. Show how to spread glue with a cotton swab on the chair and sprinkle glitter on it.

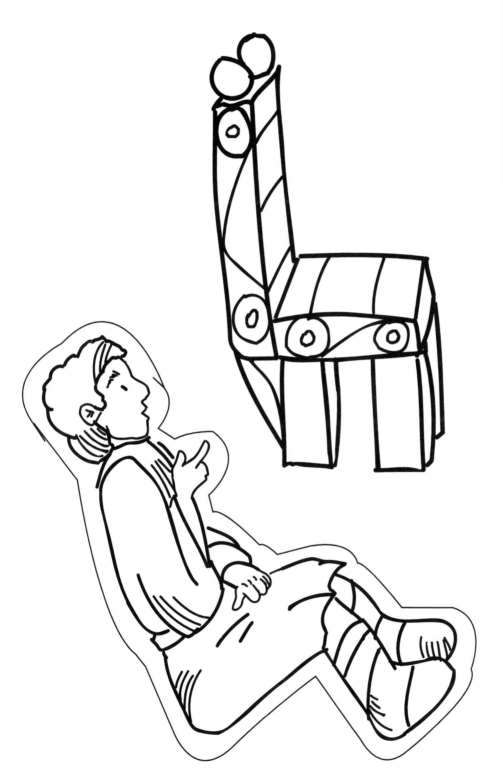

David Teaches Me to Be Caring

activity

Materials
- small crowns
- glue
- cotton swabs
- glitter
- poster board
- camera
- markers

Directions
1. Before class, duplicate and cut out a crown for each child.
2. Write "Our Caring Class" at the top of the poster board. Write the memory verse at the bottom.
3. Take pictures of students helping each other.
4. Instruct the children to spread glue on the crowns and sprinkle them with glitter.
5. Glue the pictures to the poster. Fill in the empty spaces with glitter crowns.

David Teaches Me to Be Caring

Our Caring Class Poster

finished poster

Hand Me the Scepter

· · · · · · · · · ·

Materials
- star
- craft sticks
- glue
- 1/4 cup flour
- 1/4 cup salt
- 1/4 cup water
- yellow tempera paint
- paint brushes
- paint smocks

Directions
1. Before class, duplicate and cut out two stars per student.
2. Mix the flour, salt, water and tempera paint together.
3. Allow the children to paint the stars.
4. Glue the stars together with a craft stick in the middle.
5. Play the game.

"I'm The King" Relay
Divide the class into two teams. Line the children in single file lines and give the first in line a scepter. Stand five feet from the two lines. Instruct the first one in line to run to you, touch your hand with the scepter, then run back and hand the scepter to the next in line, continuing until one team finishes.

Chapter 8

Philip Teaches Me to Tell Others About Jesus

Memory Verse

Go…and preach the good news. Mark 16:15

Story to Share
I'll Tell You About Jesus

Philip was preaching in the city of Samaria. He was telling the people there about Jesus. "You can have your sins forgiven," he told them.

Many people believed what Philip told them and asked Jesus to forgive their sins. Philip was anointed by God to work many miracles. People who couldn't move were able to walk and sick people became well. The people of Samaria were very happy.

Philip enjoyed preaching to the Samaritans. It was a wonderful thing to preach and have people respond. But one day an angel appeared to Philip.

The angel said, "God wants you to leave Samaria and take the road which goes down from Jerusalem to Gaza. Take that road to the desert."

Philip didn't hesitate to obey what God said. He left right away. When he arrived at the place, Philip saw an important man from Ethiopia in a chariot. When the man came closer, Philip saw that he was reading the book from the Bible called Isaiah.

Philip ran over to the man. "Do you understand what you are reading?"

"No," answered the Ethiopian. "And I don't have anyone to tell me. Can you sit up here in my chariot and explain to me what I am reading?"

So Philip sat in the chariot and began telling the man about Jesus. "He came to earth as a baby, He was a man without sin, yet the Jews crucified Him. When Jesus died on the cross, He died for your sins so that all you need to do is ask for forgiveness."

The Ethiopian man was overjoyed. "I believe," he said. "I believe that Jesus Christ is the Son of God and that He can save my sins. Thank you, Philip, for telling me the good news."

— based on Acts 8:26-39

Questions for Discussion
1. What would have happened if Philip had not obeyed God?
2. Is obedience important?

Tell the Good News

song

• • • • • • • • • • •

Materials
- rectangle patterns
- construction paper
- glue

Directions

1. Duplicate the patterns, trace them onto construction paper and cut out two per child.
2. Show how to glue the two rectangles together to form a cross.
3. Instruct them to hold hands and form a circle. Choose one child to be inside the circle.
4. Sing the song to the tune of "Oh the More We Get Together."
5. The child inside the circle chooses someone to tell about Jesus by handing over the cross. That child joins him in the center of the circle, handing his cross to someone while singing the song the second time. Continue until all have given their crosses away. The last one should hand the cross to the first one in the circle.

Song

Oh, I want to be like Philip,
like Philip, like Philip.
Oh, I want to be like Philip,
And tell the good news.
Good news about Jesus,
who died to save us,
Oh, I want to be like Philip,
And tell the good news.

I'll tell _____ the good news,
the good news, the good news.
I'll tell _____ the good news.
Good news of God's love.

Good News Tattoos

craft

. . . .
Materials

- symbol patterns
- white tissue paper
- water-based markers
- damp cloth

Directions

1. Before class, cut out the patterns from tissue paper for each child.
2. Allow the children to color the patterns with markers in their choices of colors.
3. Lay a pattern, marker side down, on a child's arm. Cover with a damp cloth. Lift away the tissue, leaving the tattoo.
4. Say, **These symbols will remind you to tell the good news of Jesus to others. You can say, "This reminds me of the good news of Jesus."**
5. If time permits, allow the children to practice telling their classmates about Jesus.

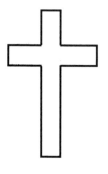

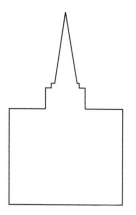

Salt Painted Chariot

craft

Materials
- chariot and ribbon
- liquid starch
- water
- yellow tempera paint
- paintbrushes
- paint smocks
- salt
- glue
- yarn
- hole punch

Directions
1. Duplicate and cut out a chariot and ribbon for each child. Punch a hole in the top of the chariot.
2. Mix 1/4 cup starch, 1/4 cup water and two tablespoons of yellow tempera paint together. Pour the mixture into small containers.
3. Help the children into paint smocks. Allow them to paint the chariot.
4. Give each child a pinch of salt to sprinkle over the painted chariot.
5. Instruct the children to glue the ribbon to the bottom of the chariot.
6. Tie a yarn hanger through the tops.
7. Say, **Hang this in your window to remind you to tell others the good news of Jesus.**

Go…and preach the good news. Mark 16:15

GO AND PREACH

Handing Out the Good News

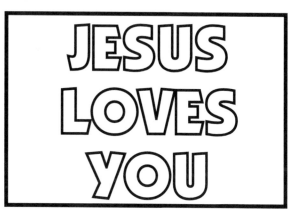

Materials
- tag and note
- toilet tissue tubes
- candy
- tissue paper
- ribbon
- crayons

Directions
1. Before class, duplicate and cut out a tag and note for each child. Cut the tissue tubes in half.
2. Allow the children to color the notes.
3. Instruct them to fold the verse and put it in the tube along with some candy.
4. Show how to wrap the tube with tissue paper and assist in tying the ends with ribbon.
5. Instruct the children to glue the "Good News" tag on the front.
6. Say, **In England people call these "crackers" because they crack with a loud pop when they are opened. This is a "quiet" good news cracker. Give your good news cracker to someone who doesn't know Jesus and share the good news!**

Philip Teaches Me to Tell Others About Jesus

Match the Chariots

Materials

- activity sheet
- crayons

Directions

1. Before class, duplicate the activity sheet for each child.
2. Instruct the children to match the chariots.
3. Allow them to color the matching chariots the same color.

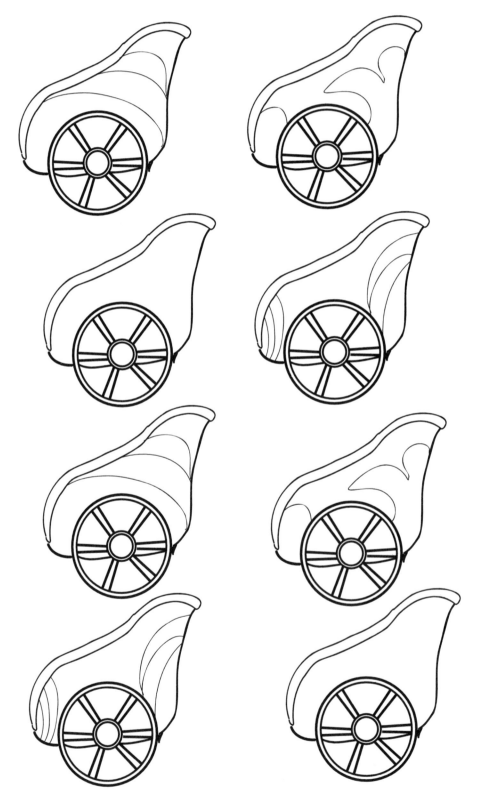

Are You Telling the Good News?

activity

· · · · · · · · · ·

Materials
- activity sheet
- crayons

Directions
1. Before class, duplicate the activity sheet for each child.
2. Say, **How you act tells others if you love Jesus. Circle the children who look like they love Jesus.**
3. Allow the children to color the pictures.

Chariot Wheels

snack

Materials

- placemat
- clear, self-stick paper
- round crackers
- peanut butter
- shoestring licorice
- plastic knives

Directions

1. Before class, duplicate and cut out the placemat for each child and cover them with clear, self-stick plastic. Cut the licorice into 1" pieces.
2. Instruct the children to spread peanut butter on the crackers.
3. Demonstrate how to lay the licorice on the crackers to look like spokes.
4. Show the children where to lay their cracker wheels to complete the placemat.

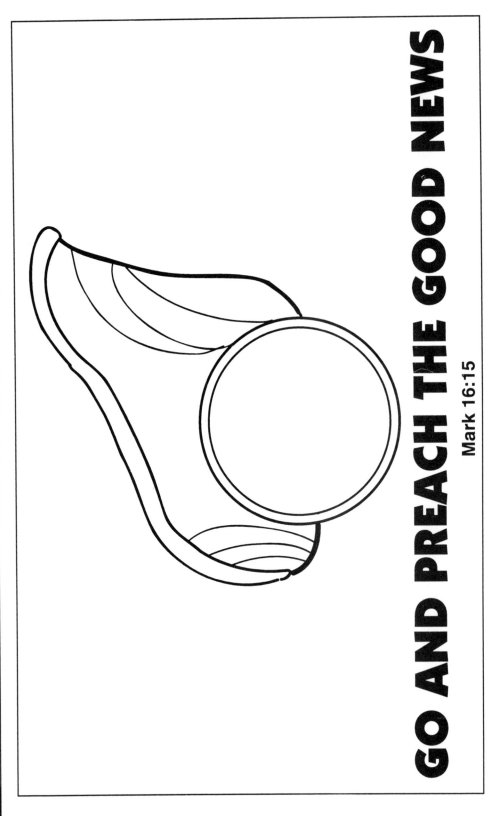

GO AND PREACH THE GOOD NEWS

Mark 16:15

Chariot Race

game

. . . .

Materials

- Philip figure
- crayons
- clothesline
- spring-type clothespins

Directions

1. Before class, duplicate and cut out a Philip for each child.
2. Allow the children to color Philip.
3. Stretch a clothesline across the room, low enough that your preschoolers can reach it.
4. Help the students clip their Philips on the clothesline with a clothespin.
5. Instruct them to pick a friend.
6. Have the children hold on to each other with their hands on their elbows.
7. Say, "Go and preach the good news" then have a team race to the clothesline, each pick off a Philip and race back. The first team home wins.
8. If you have limited space, use a stop watch and time each team.

Philip Teaches Me to Tell Others About Jesus

Chapter 9
Miscellaneous Activities

Sing to the tune of "Rise and Shine":

Clap your hands and be willing servants (servants),
Clap your hands and be willing servants (servants),
Clap your hands and be willing servants,
Living for the Lord.

Clap your hands and serve like Joshua,
Clap your hands and serve like Joshua,
Clap your hands and serve like Joshua,
Learning to be brave.

Clap your hands and serve like Nehemiah, (repeat)
Learning to be fair.

Clap your hands and serve like Stephen, (repeat)
Learning to forgive.

Clap your hands and serve like the wise men,
(repeat)
Learning to be giving.

Clap your hands and serve like Ruth, (repeat)
Learning to be thankful.

Clap your hands and serve like Aaron, (repeat)
Learning to be helpful.

Clap your hands and serve like David, (repeat)
Learning to be caring.

Clap your hands and serve like Philip, (repeat)
Sharing the good news.

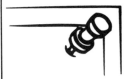

bulletin board

• • • • • • • • • • •

Materials

- star patterns
- blue paper
- yarn
- yellow paper

Directions

1. Cover the bulletin board with blue paper. Duplicate and cut out stars from yellow paper.
2. Freehand cut or trace lettering that says "God's Servants." Attach it to the middle of the board.
3. Attach eight pieces of yarn from the title outward.
4. Sing the song "Be Willing Servants" and choose a child to put one of God's servants at the end of one of the yarn pieces as you sing the applicable verse.
5. You may glue the children's pictures to the stars and attach them to the board around the Bible characters.
6. At the end of the lesson ask each child who they would like to be like. Make tags saying, "Brave Jordan," "Helpful Hannah," etc. to put under the pictures.

God's Servants

finished bulletin board

activity

Directions

1. Read the poem and do the hand motions slowly for the children.
2. Invite them to join you as you repeat it.

Wiggle Buster for God's Servants

I'm God's servant.
point to top of head

I can reach for the sky,
stretch arms toward sky

And fly, fly, fly.
flap arms

I can give a big sigh,
deep breath

And wave good-bye.
wave with both hands

Oh me, oh me, oh my.
slowly dropping head on chest

I'm God's servant.
sit down

God's Servant Certificate

Materials
- certificate and bee
- yellow paper
- glue
- glitter chenille wire
- unsharpened pencils

Directions
1. Before class, duplicate and cut out a certificate from white paper and a bee from yellow paper for each child. Cut the chenille wire into thirds. Fill in the blanks on the certificate.
2. Demonstrate how to curl the ends of a chenille wire on a pencil.
3. Show where to glue these chenille wire antennae on the bee.
4. Instruct the children to glue the bee to the certificate.

Miscellaneous Activities

This is to certify that

_____

has promised to

BEE

God's Servant

Date _____

Teacher _____

Help!

teacher help

• • • • • • • • • •

Directions

1. Duplicate and cut out the note.
2. Check off the items you needs and insert the date on the blank line when you want them brought in. You may issue one note at the beginning of the eight lessons or issue one note per week or every few weeks, depending on your needs.

Dear Parents,

The friends from class _____ need your help.

> Sometimes our tummies growl,
> And our faces are so sad.
> If you provide our snacks,
> We will be so very glad!

Items needed:

❏ marshmallows, large and small
❏ mini candy-coated chocolate pieces
❏ powdered sugar
❏ corn syrup
❏ popcorn
❏ cookie sprinkles
❏ raisins
❏ round crackers

❏ chocolate chips
❏ peanut butter
❏ dry milk
❏ mini chocolate chips
❏ pudding
❏ mini cookies
❏ pretzels
❏ shoestring licorice

Please have your donation in by

_____

Yes, I will help by bringing

_____

Parent of _____

activity

••••••••••••

Directions

1. Read the questions to the class and see who can answer first.
2. Include more information about each character when necessary if the children become stumped.

Who Am I? Review

I'm God's servant.
I am very thankful for the food God gave to me.
"Give thanks to him" is my theme.
Who am I? (Ruth)

I'm God's servant.
I was Moses' helper, with some help from Hur,
Because we wanted to "Be devoted to one another."
Who am I? (Aaron)

I'm God's servant.
My friend's son Mephibosheth was lame in both feet.
To "Show Compassion" I sat him at my table to eat.
Who am I? (King David)

I'm God's servant.
"Go...and preach the good news" out in the desert hot.
I found a man in a chariot who wanted to be taught.
Who am I? (Philip)

I'm God's servant.
"It's time to fight the Canaanites," God said to me.
"Do not fear," He told me. "You'll win the victory."
Who am I? (Joshua)

I'm God's servant.
They hated my preaching so started throwing stones.
I quietly "Forgave and the Lord forgave me" as they broke my bones.
Who am I? (Stephen)

I'm God's servant.
We brought gifts to baby Jesus, as happy as could be.
For "God loves a cheerful giver" is the giver's key.
Who are we? (wise men)

I'm God's servant.
I taught the rich men to "Bear with each other."
Building, building, building; everyone was fair.
Who am I? (Nehemiah)